What's the Matter with Christy?

The Best in Wholesome Reading
DISTRIBUTED BY:
CHOICE BOOKS OF SOUTHEAST
P. O. BOX 7525
SARASOTA, FLORIDA 33578
WE WELCOME YOUR RESPONSE

What's the Matter with Christy?

Ruth Allen

BETHANY HOUSE PUBLISHERS
MINNEAPOLIS, MINNESOTA 55438
A Division of Bethany Fellowship, Inc.

Copyright © 1982
Ruth Allen
All rights reserved

Published by Bethany House Publishers
A Division of Bethany Fellowship, Inc.
6820 Auto Club Road, Minneapolis, Minnesota 55438

Printed in the United States of America

Library of Congress Cataloging in Publication Data
Allen, Ruth.
    What's the matter with Christy?
    1.Mothers and daughters. 2.Pregnant schoolgirls. 3.Teen-age marriage. I.Title.
HQ755.85.A43 1982   248.8'431   82-8036
ISBN 0-87123-629-X   AACR2

Dedication

For Christina Robin and her parents

Contents

What's the Matter with Christy? 9
Wedding Plans 35
I Take Thee 57
Letting Go 67
Anticipation 87
The Baby 97
Epilogue 109

What's the Matter with Christy?

January 7

Here I am again, God. I'm worried about Christy. She's not herself these days. She's pale and listless; instead of bouncing through the house, she's dragging herself from chair to chair and taking naps.

Maybe she has the flu, or maybe it's mononucleosis. Should I call the doctor? Please don't let it be anything earth-shattering, Lord!

Christmas vacation is over, and my life has just now taken on a semblance of orderliness. Ann, our oldest daughter, has finally found a job. She had come home again after being on her own for a while and after a painful romance. Her misery has penetrated deep inside of me, hurting me too.

Our second child, Tim, who has had an emotional and physical dependency, moved into a halfway house where we hope he will be able to find his way back into society. They've both been through so much, but deep within I know that God loves Ann and Tim. He has a special plan for both of them. I wonder what it is? I pray that they will not miss it.

Elizabeth has returned to her Christian college. I hope everything goes well for her there. Stephanie and Christy are back in high school, and Phillip in grade school. Life is good today. I am glad the holidays are over and I have this house to myself. I can think my own quiet thoughts and not argue with anyone or worry about anybody—that is, except for Christy. I wonder why she's so listless?

January 11

Yes, it's been a good week. I finished the articles for our church magazine. Ann seems to like her job and Tim is getting along all right at the halfway house.

But I'm still worried about Christy. I went to watch her play basketball. She wasn't herself at all. She didn't "hustle" the way she usually does, and the coach took her out after the first quarter. She looked pale and told me later that she felt weak. But she wasn't too weak to go out with Todd afterwards. I like him all right, but he's two and a half years older than Christy. Besides that, I still think she's too young to be dating anyone yet.

Two years ago when she wanted to go to Homecoming with Todd, she was only thirteen and in eighth grade. She was afraid to ask me herself, so she had her older sister approach me one hour before Todd was to pick her up! I replied, "No, Ann, Tim and Elizabeth didn't date until they were sixteen, and Stephanie and Christy aren't going to either."

All four of the older children chimed in with, "Let her, Mom! Let her." So I gave in, and I've been giving in ever since.

January 13

This morning I went to my Bible study group, but I couldn't keep my mind on the study. I haven't gotten hold of Dr. Peterson yet, and all I could think about was Christy.

Why is she so listless and pale? Could she have mononucleosis, or something really terrible like leukemia? Or could she be....

Oh, no, God! She can't be pregnant!

January 14

I decided on my approach: this morning I joked to Christy, "You're sure dragging around here like an old pregnant lady!" but she didn't pick up on it at all, either in response or reaction. Surely she would want to tell me if she were.

She can't be pregnant! Todd's mother and I are good friends, and we've been strict with them. For a long time we allowed them only one date a week; but, then, they always ended up together, anyway, in group activities. When they go out they usually go to a movie or a ball game, then to the pizza place and are home on time. But when they go bike riding with ten other kids, they often do arrive home a little later than the rest.

I've talked very plainly to our four girls about dating, about emotions that get progressively stronger and stronger. And I've tried to talk to Christy about her increasing involvement with Todd; but she has a way of putting me off and making me feel that everything is okay.

No, she couldn't be that involved. She's too wise, too good for that.

January 15

Today I couldn't concentrate on anything, so I went to drink coffee with a friend. It didn't help at all.

I went home and called my doctor's office again; he was there and I talked to him. He suggested I have her come in and they would run a pregnancy test. So I made an appointment for Christy and called her home from school.

Christy wanted to know why I had her come home and why the doctor's appointment. I told her.

She got all red and flustered and said, "But, Mom, we've been careful!"

My heart sank. They have been having a sexual relationship. I am sure she is pregnant.

I wanted to yell and holler at her and remind her of the times I tried to get really serious with her about their relationship and how she would answer, "It's okay, Mom. We know what we're doing." Yes, they knew what they were doing, all right! If only I had pressed her....

But, anyway, I know she doesn't need to be torn down. She will be needing our support and forgiveness.

Oh, how I wish my husband were at home and we could talk! He's at a pastors' conference and won't be home until tomorrow night.

Christy didn't want me with her at the clinic. She was there for over an hour. Panic raced through me, and I couldn't do anything but pace around the house and stare at the walls.

Finally I couldn't stand the waiting any longer. I decided to go to the clinic. She was still in the waiting room. I could tell she still didn't want me there with her, so I left. As I left the clinic I met Todd's mother. She asked if someone was sick. I looked directly at her and said, "I hope not."

She said, "Oh, no!"

We both went to her house and anguished together.

After a while I returned to the clinic. This time Christy asked me to stay, and I went into the examining room with her. The doctor said the test was positive, and she asked me what that meant. I told her it meant that she was pregnant. A tear rolled down her cheek.

I told her that didn't mean she was a bad girl, but it did mean that we had big problems.

Oh, God! There is so much pain inside me.

I am no stranger to trouble—it seems as though I never have been. There's always been physical and mental suffering of some kind for me. But now life is upside down, and it seems as though it will never be right side up.

This is such a bitter disappointment, Lord! Christy's just fifteen; she's just a baby! My precious little girl—pregnant! I don't know what we're going to do.

Right now I can think of so many things we might have done differently. We should never have let her go out on that first date with him. Why didn't we insist? Because we didn't want to fight with her. What a price to pay for keeping the peace!

Why, Lord? Why does my heart ache so? I wonder about me. Is it because of me that some of our children have chosen to walk on paths of rebellion and pain? That one nightmare follows another?

This pain is too much to bear. I don't know how I can live through another day. Oh, Lord, where ARE You in the midst of my misery and tears?

But, I remember that in the past there were darker days than this one. Through physical and mental illness, through emotional torment, You calmed me and gave me peace and strength that I never knew existed. You have brought me through many stormy seas and troubled waters.

I look to You now, Lord. Help me! Help us!

January 16

I am numb from crying. My brain hurts from thinking so hard. I try to dream up solutions that just aren't there.

Oh, how I ache for Christy! My youngest daughter bursting with beauty and talent—now stifled.

I can understand why people think abortion would be an easy way out. But we do not have the option to snuff out a life; all of us consider abortion to be murder. Anyway, Christy wants to marry Todd and keep the baby. But they are so young. Do we solve one problem by creating another?

Even in the midst of my pain, there is joy. My children pray to God and minister to me in so many ways. When I called Elizabeth at college and told her, she cried. Then she said, "Mom, God works in many different ways. I'll be praying for all of you."

When I told Stephanie, she went to the piano and played her heart out. Tears ran down her cheeks as she said, "Mom, you know God can use even this."

I am worried about my husband, Tom. When I told him about Christy, he just hung his head and didn't say anything. He hurts but he doesn't shed tears and he can't talk about it. It grieves me to see him this way.

Later Tom asked, "How can I preach and teach . . . ?" He didn't even finish the sentence, but I think it goes like this, ". . . when I can't even raise my own family?" We really do feel like failures as parents.

Are You there, Lord? Are You truly real? Hear the pleadings of my heart. Soothe the pain. Guide us and show us what to do.

January 17

Tonight we went again to see her play basketball. I knew it would be the last game she would ever play. She didn't start and only played for less than a quarter.

I had a lump in my throat and a burning in my chest. I felt like I wanted to throw up, and I was sure I didn't have the flu. A casual friend sat next to me and talked and talked. I couldn't concentrate enough to know what she was talking about, but I tried to give her appropriate answers. I clapped when everyone else did, but I couldn't yell.

It must have been as hard for Tom as it was for me. Every now and then he squeezed my hand and I squeezed his. We gave each other comfort and courage.

I keep wondering if anybody knows. I can't imagine what it will be like when the news leaks out. I think I would like to take a long vacation to Tibet or New Zealand.

January 18

This morning a close friend called me on the phone and asked me to come for coffee. I couldn't stand to face anyone, so I told her I didn't have a car. Then I retreated into myself to mourn some more.

She called back and said she was coming to get me. When we arrived at her house, another close friend was there, too.

They said I didn't look well. I couldn't hold back my tears any longer. I told them Christy was pregnant. They were very supportive. It made me feel better.

Then we went to see another very close friend—someone with whom I have shared much in the last five years. When I told her Christy was pregnant, she said, "Ruth, I have something to tell you. Our Melissa is pregnant, too. And we don't know what we or the kids are going to do."

We all cried together. Sharing our suffering with each other surely has lightened our burdens.

Todd is coming over tonight. I have never disliked him. It's just that I haven't liked her dating *anyone* these past two years, especially someone two and a half years older than her. I shouldn't have ever let her go with him, but I thought I couldn't bear to fight with her. I had battled so much with Ann that I couldn't face that struggle with another child.

Lord, if they get married, then Todd will be a member of our family. Help me to have the same kind of feelings for him that I have for Christy and my other children. And let me be supportive of him and have sympathy for his own unique situation.

Help me now in this new relationship.

When Todd came through the door and sat down in our living room, I wanted to strike out and say something cruel. But God helped me. I put my arm around his shoulder and hugged him. Because my own sins are forgiven, I was able to reach out in love and embrace him.

January 19

Tonight Todd's mother called me on the phone and asked us to come over.

Todd and Christy, Todd's parents, and Tom and I all sat down together and discussed the options. The first one we considered is that Christy could give up the baby for adoption and they would stop seeing each other. None of us is very happy with this choice. I knew of a young girl who gave up her baby; then, a year later, the couple got married, and they didn't have their baby. Could giving up the baby hurt Christy and Todd for a lifetime?

The second option is that Christy could have the baby and keep it; then wait and get married in two years when she graduates. But will they stop their physical relationship because we think they should? In this situation, that does not seem likely.

Then we discussed Christy giving the baby up for adoption and going away to boarding school until they get over each other. But Christy and Todd are sure they will never "get over each other." If we force them apart, will Christy hate us forever?

We talked about the "ifs" and "maybes" but came to no final conclusions. We decided that the kids should see a counselor. None of us tried to place the blame on anyone. We parents were supportive of our children.

God, if they do get married, their chances of making it will be so much greater if we can remain supportive. So show us how to stand behind them.

January 20

Lord, I don't understand it. I really do have such joy again, even when everything is supposedly dark.

What am I celebrating? Is it Your faithfulness, God? Is it knowing You are there, waiting to call my name? Is it because You give me strength when I am weak? Do I celebrate because You feed me when I hunger and give cold drink when I thirst? Is it because You cause joy to abound even when I am depressed?

Right now it is difficult with my mind's eye to see any good in this situation. Can good come even from this?

I am confused. I feel like I don't know things that I should know. I don't know the answers; I don't even know the questions.

When I run, I fall. When I walk, I stumble. When I swim, I sink. I feel like a failure.

But I celebrate today because You know my name.

January 23

So life goes on. The world didn't stop. I no longer feel like crying all the time. Sometimes I just feel undone—kind of restless and crabby. I guess I'm getting somewhat used to this hurtful predicament.

I still want to ask, "Why Christy?" She's always been such a good daughter—kind and helpful, with a cheerfulness that is contagious. How happy she made me the day she was born! And she's been cheering me ever since. I've been so proud when she has sung solos with the school chorus and in church. It's been exciting to watch her run the 880 in track and play basketball. She does things like cleaning and dishes without being asked. And she's been so serious about her faith in God—believing and living it.

Why, Lord? Why do troubles stalk us and we fall easy prey? Is it because the evil one is a reality and awaits us at every turn? Is it because we are not aware of the little choices which make openings for sin in our lives?

January 26

Christy went to the clinic today for some blood tests. Other patients were there, too. I wonder if people are guessing.

I don't want people to know right away. I guess I don't want to talk about it—at least until we know what is decided on, what our course of action will be. The whole thing makes me very uncomfortable in public and pains me in private.

I think it would be hard for Christy, too, if people knew right now. Her friends would ask, "Are you going to get married?" and she'd have to answer, "I don't know" or "I think so" or "If our parents let us."

I want everything to be settled right now. I feel frustrated and impatient with the uncertainty, but we must be patient. If we make hasty decisions, we all might regret them.

Lord, help us to "hang loose" and wait on You to lead us to wise decisions.

January 27

To be honest, I wish Christy would have a miscarriage. Abortion is wrong, but, if she would only miscarry naturally! She is too young to be thinking of marriage and a family. I want her life to go on uninterrupted—school, music, sports and church. Even her church life will be different if she's married. She won't be a part of our Christian youth group.

I'm not numb anymore. Reality has set in, and I just ache a little all over. We still don't know what is going to happen. They will be seeing a counselor to discuss marriage and other alternatives. They want so much to be married, but we're not sure. Marriage is for a lifetime. Do they realize how long a lifetime is? Are they ready for that?

Neither Christy nor Todd want to give the baby up for adoption. To tell the truth, I don't want them to either. If the decision were only mine right now, I would say she should keep the baby and get married to Todd after she graduates from high school.

I'm glad they can't be married for at least two months, not until after her sixteenth birthday. It gives all of us time—time for decisions and time to plan. Time for wisdom—I hope.

Lord, give us strength to face each day squarely. Help us to deal honestly with life and in love toward each other.

February 4

We talked with the marriage counselor with whom they've met twice. He feels that marriage is probably the best solution "for right now." He's a Christian and believes that marriages should last a lifetime, so I wonder what he meant by "right now." Maybe he meant to say "in this situation." I wish I could have talked to him some more, but we had already talked too long and he was late for his next appointment.

I wanted to hear him say that they're very mature for their age and have a good chance of "living happily ever after."

Lord, I realize that the other alternatives aren't that terrific either, so help me to accept this solution. Help us to help them make it work.

Tonight we sat down with Christy and Todd and his parents and talked again. We all agree that marriage seems the best alternative, especially since they obviously care for each other. The wedding date is finally set.

I don't want to admit it, but I find myself strangely joyful now. They are so happy about each other and their happiness is contagious.

Yes, I even feel happy about the baby. I can't imagine what he or she will look like. I can't imagine us being grandparents. I have come to the place that part of me wishes I could shout to the world that we're going to have our first grandchild; but yet still can hardly bring myself to tell our closest friends. I'm afraid of what people might think and say—not just about me or our family, but about Christy. Will they be understanding and kind? Soon the whispers and knowing glances will start, and I cringe at that.

I wish things didn't have to be this way. Again, I feel pulled in two directions: on the one hand, I wish we could really celebrate and plan a big wedding. Christy wants one. But a formal fanfare just doesn't "sit right" with us or with Todd's folks. It makes us feel uncomfortable. We wonder if it would be "proper." Is it our selfishness and fear of criticism that makes us want to be proper? We want their wedding to be a sacred event, but yet we don't want to celebrate the breaking of God's law. I feel like wearing two signs to the wedding: the one on my chest could read, "*We give them our blessing*," and the one on my back would say, "*But it's still not right.*"

> *Lord, a wedding is a once-in-a-lifetime event. How do you want this important occasion solemnized? Help us to do the right thing for our children.*

February 5

Underneath it all, I still don't know for sure if our decision to let Christy and Todd get married is a wise one. I just don't have the confidence about it that I would like to have. I wish God would give me some unmistakable sign; and I wish He could issue me a written guarantee saying they will live happily ever after.

We've debated the alternatives so many times, and marriage does seem to be the most reasonable. My problem is that I am not reasonable—I want her life to go on the way it was before.

Lord, help me to quit dragging my feet; help me to accept—yes, and be happy—with this decision. And help me to give them my blessing without reservation. Isn't that the way You bless us?

February 6

I have many opposing feelings today. Resentment, fear of criticism, and disappointment are all mixed up with a sprinkling of love, joy, and thankfulness.

Right now I am happy because Christy says she plans to finish high school, uninterrupted except for two weeks in September when the baby is born. She sounds enthusiastic, even eager; and, further, says she still plans on college. But I wonder. She can set her sights high, but she can't know the involvement, time and energy it takes to make a home and be a mother.

I know this daughter of mine. She will take joy in making her home and give it her all. I wonder if there will be enough interest and energy left over for discovering and becoming.

I have had such dreams for her. She is blessed with an abundance of raw talent. Will much of it even be discovered? utilized?

I must cast off these feelings of melancholy about her future and be joyful for the present. I do realize that we have much to be thankful for. Todd is a fine person, and we are friends with his family. Christy does still plan on completing her education. And they seem to be serious and sensible about getting their future in order.

God, be with Christy and Todd as they plan on what they will do and what they will not do. Be with them as they think about who they are and who they will become. Bless them as they plan their life together.

February 7

People *are* whispering, and I don't like it. I want to be open but I don't know how. We've finally told all of our closest friends, but I don't feel like talking about such sensitive matters with every acquaintance I meet on the street.

Perhaps we should announce the wedding formally in the newspaper so people will stop speculating about what's going on. If we announce it in the paper does that make it seem like we are proud of what's happened? I just don't know how we should handle this.

I do know one thing: we will not pretend that everything is fine, that we approve of a fifteen-year-old getting married. We will tell people that it does hurt, but that we love our daughter and the boy she has chosen to be her life partner. We will tell them that we don't believe what Christy and Todd did was right, but that they are still fine, good young people. We will tell them that we expect the kids and us, their parents, to make the best of it.

Lord, during this coming week the news of our daughter and Todd will flit over many tongues. Help me not to cringe as I meet people.

I realize now that this is not a "cosmic" event—though in our little town it might seem like it! I need not stutter and turn tail as I acknowledge this painful situation.

Give me courage, and help me to be able to keep on giving my blessing to these young people whom I love.

February 8

For the last month I have been so involved with Christy that I have forgotten the other children in our home.

My mind has been spinning and my emotions spilling out as we have attempted to work through this dilemma. So much so that I hardly notice another child or hear a question asked.

I know that Ann, Timothy, Elizabeth, Stephanie, and Phillip continue to have needs. They still need a listening ear. They, too, feel pain and disappointment for a sister. They still need to be recognized and to feel our support. They need to know that we appreciate their strivings, their accomplishments, their loyalty and steadfastness.

Lord, forgive me for my shortsightedness. Bring me back on course. Help me to get things in proper perspective. Open my eyes to be aware of ALL of the needs in our family. Make me sensitive to each one of my children in these trying days. And to Tom, Lord, also. Show us both ways to encourage and support each other.

Wedding Plans

February 16

Today I feel happy—almost exuberant—about everything. Christy and I went shopping for her wedding dress. Her sisters and Todd's mother went, too, and we all got excited looking at patterns and materials.

She's going to be an old-fashioned bride in gauze and lace. Her sisters will wear flowered gauze with matching scarves and they'll be carrying baskets of flowers.

I do want Christy to have a beautiful wedding. Some may think she doesn't deserve it; but we believe and hope and pray her marriage will last a lifetime, and I don't want any regrets. I want her wedding day to be a cherished day that she will remember fondly fifty years from now.

It was such fun shopping this afternoon and making plans! His mother has offered to sew her dress, and I will make the bridesmaids' dresses.

God, all of a sudden I feel almost giddy with joy, and scared too—scared as I realize how much preparation awaits me this coming month.

Please, Lord, help me to be strong and organized, and happy.

February 18

We sat down last night with Christy and Todd and his folks to plan the wedding service. We sifted through thoughts and ideas until we came up with one that all of us could be happy about.

The wedding will be traditional and reverent. Only our closest friends and relatives will share this hallowed hour of our children's lives. We will drink the cup and eat the bread and together experience the forgiveness of sins. When we leave the altar it will be a time of new beginnings for them and for us.

There will be no trivia in our Lord's house. All of the music will be very sacred as we ask God's blessing on our children. We will surround Christy and Todd with our love and prayers as they pledge their lives to each other.

Lord, help us now as we prepare for the wedding. Help us to celebrate love, and life, and Your faithfulness.

Let us offer up a service that is pleasing to You, one that You will honor with Your blessing and presence.

February 21

It really bothers me that Christy doesn't seem to think they did anything wrong. I've also talked with the other girls and some of their friends about having sex outside of marriage, and the prevailing attitude seems to be, "It's okay if you love each other."

Am I archaic?—out of touch with today's reality? Do I interpret God's Word with a narrow mind?

I believe that whenever we depart from the authority of the Bible, we are left at the mercy of the winds of fate. When we try to cast off God's Word, where in this world do we find a standard? Left to ourselves, human discernment of right and wrong varies with the whims of culture, and circumstance.

They say, "It's okay if you love each other." What is love? Is it a biological urge, or tender caring? Is it a self-centered act, or giving of self? Is it momentary madness or eternal dedication? Is it free or does it involve responsibility? Is love responsible for an unborn child or the vulnerability of a bared soul? Did God have a good reason for keeping sex only in the framework of marriage?

Your Word, O Lord, is as true and as workable as it was two thousand years ago. Help me and my loved ones to embrace the authority of Your Word for our lives now.

Forgive us for the times when we feel that our ideas and ideals for humanity are better than Your divine plan.

Father, I believe that You designed marriage to be the circle to support, to contain, sexual intimacy. Help me to present this truth in a convincing manner to my children and their friends.

February 22

Today I don't know how to pray or even what to to wish for.

I came home this afternoon to find Christy in bed. She told me that she had had severe cramps all day and had called the doctor. He told her to stay in bed with her legs elevated. She is afraid she is going to miscarry.

I don't understand it! If I were pregnant and only fifteen years old and not married, I might be horse jumping or taking castor oil—anything to make a miscarriage happen.

While I talked to Christy, tears rolled from her eyes and she pleaded, "Mom, can we still get married if. . . ?"

I am used to the idea of them getting married now. Sometimes I have even felt excited about the wedding; but if I could do the choosing, I know I would opt for Christy to remain at home as our youngest daughter. I would choose for her to stay in that special spot in our home and our hearts reserved only for her.

But can we go back? Can things ever be the same?

If there were no wedding, a whole new set of problems would be ours. Would they discontinue a sexual relationship because their parents disapproved? Not likely. They still are not convinced. Would we be tempted to send her away to school so we could separate them? What kind of alienation would that bring in our home?

Lord, I don't know how to pray. I feel confused. I am glad that this is a matter that I have no power to decide. All I can say now, God, is that Your will be done.

February 23

Christy's cramps have stopped, and she is up and about again.

I have mixed feelings: disappointment and relief. I would like to keep her home longer. I would like her to stay and share with us the panorama of her youth.

But I am also relieved that the wedding is still on and we don't have to cope with that other set of problems.

It was good to see her tears and see Todd worried. I am glad that they want the baby and are anxiously awaiting the wedding and starting their home together. Can it be that they are more ready for marriage than I think?

I feel happy that they don't seem to feel trapped into marrying each other. Their love for each other appears to be tender and real. I hope it is a forever kind of love, steady and full of hope during the tough times they will face.

February 25

Christy has been concerned about Todd these days, and I am, too. They are so happy about each other, but even I can see that he's uptight lately. Is he worried about her? Does he worry about supporting her and then a family? Do the cares of new responsibilities weigh him down?

We asked Todd if he felt trapped and reminded him that he didn't *have* to marry her. He told us he loves Christy more than anything in the world and has always wanted to marry her. But I wonder if life isn't looming too big for him right now.

Eighteen is awfully young to be saddled with so much responsibility. If only they could both continue carefree—chasing butterflies and dreams.

Todd says he has a job lined up at a gas station and that he will feel better when he gets started. He plans on working weekends and after school until eleven. Life will be so heavy for him. I wish things could have been different.

February 27

Todd is working at the gas station now and seems more relaxed.

This job will take care of their needs, but I know he doesn't like it. So I pray that he will find joy in Christy. Going to school and working will be wearisome for him. I hope he can stay strong. And I hope he will have good feelings about himself so he can be cheerful to the public and gentle with her.

From now until Todd graduates, life will be hard and heavy for him and there will be the emotional stress that comes from change. He's starting regular work, moving from his parental home, getting married, graduating, and facing fatherhood—all in a span of less than three months. I can't help but worry about him.

> *God, please don't let Todd's life get too big for him, get to be more than he can handle. Keep him well, physically, emotionally and spiritually. Let him look to You now to supply all of his needs—strength for his body, peace for his mind, and hope for his spirit. Let his soul soar high above the pettiness and trivia which will surely come his way and threaten his feeling of well-being.*
>
> *His life is full to the brim. Make his cup big enough to hold it all. Cause his days and his hours to flow smoothly and let him run with patience the race that is set before him.*

February 28

Friends of our families hosted a shower for Christy and Todd. I am overwhelmed by the love and support of so many. It seems as though the people of our community have joined us in saying to them, "Nevertheless, you *are* fine kids. We believe in you."

Almost all of her classmates were there, and they gathered close around her as she opened their gifts. With those gifts came their wishes for her happiness.

It seemed so strange to watch my little girl accepting gifts to set up housekeeping. Just yesterday she quit playing house. Now it will be for real.

God, do they know how fortunate they are to have people caring, loving, affirming, and supporting them? Most of us have to walk through a desert to appreciate the rain. They have had no desert, Lord, so help them to appreciate this shower of kindness and love, and towels and toasters.

Help them to reward the faith that kind folk have invested in them.

March 2

They haven't found a place to live yet, and the marriage counselor told them they should postpone the wedding if they can't find a place of their own. We agree that this is good advice, and there isn't a vacant apartment, trailer, or house in this whole town. I don't know what they are going to do.

>*Lord, You have promised to provide the needs of those who trust in You. I know they have looked to You; and I, too, ask You to provide a place for them to live.*
>
>*Christy told me that they have been praying to You that something will open up. They have been worried and uptight because they haven't yet discovered Your faithfulness. Help them to realize that they can count on Your being there in all of the big deals and little trivia that come their way.*
>
>*Right now help them to relax and trust in You to provide. In the meantime, we will all continue to check out any likely place that is about to become vacant.*
>
>*Direct them and us to hot leads.*

March 4

We've been so busy with sewing and baking and deciding on flowers and music. I've felt excited and exuberant for days. But today I cried through the breakfast dishes. All of a sudden I ache inside and feel miserable again.

What is the matter with me? Is my problem that I really don't want to give Christy up? That must be it. *I don't want to give her up!*

From the day she was born she has made my heart glad. She was such a funny-looking, loving child, laughing and bouncing and spilling into our lives. She's the child who senses when I am blue and acts funny to cheer me. I'm going to miss her helpfulness, too. She's never been allergic to vacuum cleaners and dishes.

I really did plan on Christy being around for almost three more years. Deep inside of me, I know I will never be ready to let her go. I want to go on forever telling her in the morning to have a good day and waiting in the evening to hear her call, "Mom, are you home?"

Lord, I realize that anytime would be too soon for Christy to leave, so help me now to let her go.

Help me not to resent Todd for taking her away too early; help me not to hold it against him because my plans have been upset.

March 6

The wedding is approaching fast, and I am feeling the beginnings of panic. Besides everything else, there is so much cleaning that needs to be done for the open-house reception.

I feel scared, like I want to run far away—did I mention New Zealand before? It is looking more and more attractive.

I can't get it all together. I don't even know where to start. People will be everywhere—upstairs, downstairs, and in the basement family room, and I want it all to be attractive and spotless.

Yesterday I tried to whip up some action around here and get everybody in the family organized and working. But they all seemed deaf, except for Stephanie. She said, "But, Mom, the wedding isn't for two weeks." Don't they realize that things like walls and curtains have to be done *now*?

Lord, I think I'm coming apart at the seams. Help me to get organized. Help me not to resent my children because they don't seem to be aware of my needs. Help me to remember how little I helped to prepare for my own wedding.

There is so much that needs to be done during these two weeks, Lord. Give me strength and organization, and, please, don't let me get sick.

And help me to realize that the world goes on around me. Don't let me get so involved in the flurry of preparation that I cease to be aware of others. I have a tendency to be sour when I am hard pressed, so help me to be cheerful.

And now, when I feel so overwhelmed with getting things done, let me serve You in love.

March 7

Today I feel like singing and dancing because Christy and Todd *have found a place to live*! I remind myself of how we all said, "Anything will do." That's exactly what they found.

I was horrified when I first saw it, but Todd's mother was optimistic. She said, "We can plasterboard the holes in the wall and put plywood over the hole in the bathroom floor. A lot of paint and a little wallpaper will do wonders."

I am happy for that miserable, beat-up old house. At least they can be married and live by themselves.

Tom and I were over there last night and I could hardly believe the activity. Their school friends were helping them, crawling all over that house, scrubbing and painting everything in sight. A friend of ours said he would help lay linoleum in the kitchen and other friends offered them an old stove and refrigerator.

> *Lord, I praise You today not only because You have provided Christy and Todd with a house but also with friends—friends who care and help and support them.*
>
> *God, throughout all of life may they continue to realize how much You love them and how You long to wonderfully supply all of their needs.*

March 9

Today my friends decided to bail me out by helping me with this house. It's embarrassing to be so disorganized that I need rescuing. I would like to believe that I am master of every situation.

But I am grateful. Four friends came over and cleaned and waxed and polished until everything shone. They gave me the big push I needed. Because they have helped me, I feel that we will be ready for the reception.

It is so difficult always being disorganized and having a large family. I never seem to know how to go about doing things that seem easy for most women.

But God always seems to know when my needs are getting to be more than I can handle. I am grateful that He has not left me alone in my chaotic condition.

Lord, thank You for these friends who have cleaned and have offered to make cookies and help with the sewing.

Thank You, God, for providing me with friends who care about what happens to me. Help me to be the same kind of a friend to others.

March 14

It was smooth sailing for days. I was excited, busy, and happy; but today is Christy's birthday, and a wave of sadness rolled over me. It knocked me down and drowned my joy.

I would like to be having a "sweet sixteen" party for her, but instead I'm preparing for her wedding.

My heart tells me she's too young to be a wife next week and then a mother. I ache to see her step from the carefree world of her childhood to the responsibility-laden realm of adulthood. But this is the consequence, the result, of their choice. So now my prayer is that God will equip her, that His grace will give her the maturity that experience has not yet had a chance to develop.

God, help her to have good feelings about herself so she can treat her husband kindly.

Give her patience to listen with interest when her husband tells her something she has already heard.

Give her warmth of personality so that her husband and others will be happy in her presence.

Give her a courageous heart when she is tossed about in the storms of life.

Give her humor when life is tedious.

Let her be filled with spirituality when all around her becomes mundane.

Give her enough energy to keep a home,

satisfy her husband, care for a child, excel in her studies, and still play tennis or ride a bike.

Help her to feel fulfilled by her husband, child, and home. But not too fulfilled, Lord. Don't let her be so content that she loses all desire for growing and becoming.

March 17

There is something that is still really bothering me. Christy and Todd have both told us that they are sorry they have embarrassed us and put us to so much trouble.

But there doesn't seem to be any evidence that they have confessed their sin to God or sought His forgiveness. Could it be that they still don't consider their sexual relationship to be sinful because they were planning to be married? Do they, too, say, "It's okay, if you love each other"?

This is a problem for me; but because God's mercy surrounds me and His grace abounds, I will still support them, still give them my blessing.

Give me wisdom, Lord, in showing my love and support to them without letting them think that I condone their sexual intimacy. Show them that what they did needs *forgiveness*, not excusing.

March 22

Tonight is the rehearsal, and tomorrow morning the wedding. Have almost three months gone by since that day I realized Christy was pregnant? Have sixteen years slipped by without my hardly noticing?

Just yesterday she was a newborn baby cradled in my arms and then she went off to kindergarten. Before I knew it she was thirteen and wanted to go to Homecoming with Todd. And tomorrow she'll be a bride. The wedding clothes are ready. So is the food, and even the house.

But am I? Are Christy and Todd?

Lord, tomorrow is a new beginning. I thank You for forgiveness in the past. Forgive me for the times I have not loved as I ought. Forgive me for the times I have failed as a mother.

Prepare me for Christy's wedding day and the breaking away of strong parental ties. Let the two of them unite strongly.

Help me to see her as a woman instead of a child. Help me to respect her privacy and recognize my limitations.

Bless the new relationships that will begin tomorrow. Help us to love him, and his parents to love her.

And, Lord, make their love for each other tender and eternal.

It was a good evening. When we sat down at the rehearsal dinner, I knew a two-day wedding celebration had begun.

After the rehearsal, some of my friends came to our house to help prepare the wedding food and the tables. When they went home, the silver service shone in anticipation and the coffeepots waited to be plugged in. Now the very house and the people in it are on tiptoe for a day of rejoicing. And I am overwhelmed. It is too wonderful having friends like these.

This is the last night my little girl will snuggle in her bed upstairs. It is the last time Christy and Stephanie will mumble to each other as they drift off to sleep. I wonder what they are saying?

Lord, I am thinking about our friends and relatives who will be rising early to drive many miles to our daughter's wedding. Grant them a safe journey.

And now I am going to bed. I am so tired. Let me find sleep so I might rise rested and ready to enjoy this memorable day of our lives.

I Take Thee

March 23

Lord, today is Christy's wedding day. I will cast off all sadness and be joyful. I will be joyful because You are here and waiting to bless us. I will celebrate Your love and faithfulness with our family and friends.

How I covet Your blessing for those who will come to the church and our home today.

Especially be with the bride and groom, Lord. Give them a quiet spirit and tenderness toward each other. As they pledge themselves to each other, I pray that You will unite with them and be the third Partner in their marriage.

I don't know exactly what today will bring, but help me to feel at peace with myself. Help me to deal capably with strong emotions that may come surging through my heart.

Now, go with me, God, and let me cherish every minute of this day.

While I was waiting for the wedding to begin, I watched our friends be seated. One by one they have come into our lives; and then, today, they were here and filed into the sanctuary to share a hallowed hour in the lives of our children.

Some of them live nearby and others travelled many miles to join with us today. Each one of them is a very special person to me. I have so many memories of them through the years.... The tears we've shed on each other's shoulders and laughter that made our sides ache; the problems discussed and the joys shared. I remember their caring and sharing and their steadfastness in good times and hard.

Through the years our friends gave us love and encouragement, and today they came to help us celebrate and share again our joy. They will help us make this occasion memorable.

What would life be like without such friends? Would a rose be beautiful if it were not shared? Can a symphony delight a lone soul? My life would lack color if it were a solo. Because of friends our joys are magnified and our sorrows made mellow.

Thank You, God, for enriching our lives with friends.

The organist played, "Jesu, Joy of Man's Desiring," and Christy walked up the aisle with her father. The other pastor asked, "Who gives this woman to be married to this man?" and her father answered, "Her mother and I." I knew she had walked out of her childhood and into womanhood.

Todd stood there waiting for Christy. The look on his face said he adored her. She was a thing of beauty—graceful and ethereal, and so very young.

They were two tender twigs being grafted together on a bough of the tree of life. Grafted together to become stronger?

> *Lord, be the trunk of that tree. Be the Supplier and the Source. You created them in the beginning. Now claim that new family unit as Your very own.*

The lump in my throat was too large too swallow when Tom gave Christy to Todd. From that moment on her allegiance was to be to her husband.

Tom then joined the other pastor, and it was his privilege to deliver his daughter's wedding sermon and join them in marriage.

He told them always to remember that their marriage was beginning at the Lord's table and in the shadow of the cross ... that the formula for love is living in forgiveness.... He told them that forgiveness heals hurts and opens up communications ... that forgiveness cleanses and embraces and makes for new beginnings.... He told them that because God forgives us, we forgive each other.

Can they know what forgiveness is all about? That sometimes it's merely saying inwardly to someone close to us, "I love you anyway, even though you are not the person I had hoped you would be."

Tom said to Christy and Todd, "If you love someone, you will be loyal to him no matter what the cost. You will believe in him, always expect the best of him, and always stand your ground in defending him."

> *Lord, help me not to stand in the way of her loyalty to her husband. Help them to un-*

derstand the words spoken to them on their wedding day.

It was a strange mixture of joy and pain that I felt during the wedding—but it was mostly joy. However, the sister closest in age to Christy, Stephanie, felt mostly pain—the pain of separation. Stephanie was Christy's Maid of Honor, and she stood there at the altar crying. She cried through the song she sang with Ann and Elizabeth, and she cried through the vows.

Her heart was heavy. For years Stephanie and Christy had been fighting and competing, but she cried through the ceremony. Was she remembering the years of playing house and dolls, and cutting out paper dolls, and having secret clubs? Born fourteen months apart, they were always together, laughing, telling secrets and jokes, arguing and challenging, sharing and caring. Fond memories robbed her of the joy of the hour.

Stephanie had so many tears, and she tried to wipe them away with her hand. Why don't bridesmaids ever think to carry handkerchiefs?

Her tears were contagious, I felt nostalgic, too. I remembered holding Christy in my arms at the front of the church when we publicly gave her to God, and now this morning she stood a bride. Todd was such a small kid—and now he stood a groom.

They pledged their love for a lifetime and were filled with love and devotion. But a sister felt naught but distress. An era of shared sister life and love was ending.

God, comfort Stephanie and us as we feel the pain of this separation.

When Christy and Todd pledged their love to each other, they promised to be faithful "as long as we both shall live." They promised to love only each other for better or worse, for richer or poorer, in sickness and in health until death do them part. Could they really promise all that?

Lord, I pray that through the years they will realize the joy of steadfastness. May their love for each other be constant through tears and laughter, excitement and boredom, and through triumphs and disappointments.

May they depend on each other for love and kindness, and for understanding when they are unhappy about themselves. And when the world seems rotten, may they find a waiting lover at home.

God, You have been with them and are with them now. So continue with them and teach them about love.

When I approached my Lord's table at the wedding today, I felt His presence more than usual. He was very near. He was waiting for me—to forgive my sins and to bless me.

Today I felt a special closeness with the others kneeling at His table. We were all the forgiven ones and He called us to be blessed. When I knelt at the altar, I felt a bond of unity with the saints who have gone on before me and those who struggle on distant ground that I've not yet walked.

> *Lord, did Christy and Todd feel Your presence, too? Keep them ever close to your heart. Live in their home and make Yourself known to them. May they look for You and find You, so that when their days on earth are used up, they and their children might be numbered among the faithful.*
>
> *Bless them so that they might become a blessing.*

How I enjoyed the reception! My joy was greater because all of the guests were important people in our lives. The friends of past decades visited with friends of here and now. The past mingled with the present and could hardly be discerned because they wore the same garment—a robe of love.

Members of two families gathered to celebrate the union of a boy and a girl who are close to our hearts. We were overwhelmed with affection for them. We wished for them happiness, health, prosperity, and a life lived according to God's will and purpose.

I'm glad we had an open-house reception. It gave us time to visit with everyone. Each person who came to our house this afternoon is a VIP in our lives. They have all loved us and they care about what happens to us. My heart embraced each one of them.

I felt like saying to them, "Thank you for being part of our lives. Thank you for being friends of our children."

Our children's friends were there, too. Will some of these friendships remain thirty or fifty years? I hope that throughout our children's lifetime they may know the joys of enduring friendships.

> *Lord, I felt sad, almost scared when they left on their honeymoon. It's more than a short wedding trip. They have embarked on the journey of shared life. Let it be a long journey, a lifetime journey.*
>
> *Bless them as they travel onward together. May they find joy in their traveling companion, zest for the wayside, and compassion for the stranger.*
>
> *God, it's an uphill journey—up rugged mountains and through rough valleys. Do go with them.*
>
> *Embrace them in Your almighty arms. Show Yourself to them and let them see how great You are. Let them see how big Your love is and how You long to supply their every need.*
>
> *Now, Lord, keep them as they honeymoon. Keep them safe on the road. Help them to have fun and delight in each other. It's a new kind of relationship for them now. They belong to each other. Help them to celebrate wedded love.*

We said good-bye to the last guests and put away the food. Then the sun slid down the western sky and all that remained of the day was a memory that has left me smiling and will gladden my old age.

Oh, God, I felt Your presence today as they spoke their vows and we all communed at Your table. You've been with us since the alarm clock interrupted the dawn and have remained even until now.

I thank You for keeping me strong through these brim-filled hours. Life overflowed today and now my bones ache, my mind is boggled, and my emotions spent . . . but my heart is warm.

It's like for months there has been nothing else going on in this whole world except this wedding. Now that it's over, I feel almost void. Tomorrow I will return borrowed dishes and things, and then what? Cleaning, and cooking, and the usual routine?

God, I thank You for the gift of this day. Help me now to pick up the pieces of an everyday world and get on with living.

Letting Go

March 26

Christy and Todd are back from their wedding trip. How exciting it is to be young. I envy their vibrancy, their expectations, their zest. The world awaits them. The future is theirs.

No shadows have fallen on their pathway. Discouragement, disillusionment, and disappointments are yet unknown to them. They are setting their life in order and planning the things they will do, the life they will lead, and who they will become.

Because I have lived, I know that life will not run on and on without a tear. I know the punctuations of anguish, disappointment, and even despair. If only they could go on like this and never suffer or experience defeat! I would that their lives could flow from one happy moment to another. But it won't. It can't.

So, God, I pray for them. Be with them now when their honeymoon is over. Bless them when misunderstandings separate, when discouragements assail them, when people interfere, when they get lazy about spiritual matters, and when they feel weary of each other.

Be there with them. You alone can offer forgiveness, heal relationships, and revitalize drab living.

March 28

I visited Christy today and she served me coffee. She is keeping her home attractive. I am glad she enjoys homemaking. She delights in her new role. Is she more ready to be a wife and a homemaker than I thought? Perhaps it is not age that qualifies a woman to create and keep a home.

I hope it isn't only the novelty of it all. I want her affection for her home to be enduring and for the making of it to continually give her joy.

Lord, may her home be a shelter for her family from the storms of life. May it be a comforting place to return to and a center of warmth for those who pass through its doors—a place where hurts are healed and all are understood.

Bless Christy and Todd. Help them to build a home that is pleasant to You.

April 3

I stopped to see Christy this afternoon, and I suddenly realized that she's a stranger in her own house. She says Todd is, too. She doesn't like to be home alone even in the daytime.

She stops often on the way home from school to sit on the couch and observe the walls. It's like she needs to bask in her childhood. And he goes to his parents' home to feel familiar things.

I guess they still need us. I have thought it might be better if they could live five hundred miles from home. But maybe strong ties aren't meant to be snapped clean.

God, it hurts to say this, but help them to pull away from us and cling to each other.

I know that their house will become their home. In time they will lend it their personality. So I pray, Lord, that they will feel comfortable inside those strange walls. Let their home surround them as a secure haven.

April 7

Sometimes I feel jealous when his mother does things for her. I am envious when I walk into church and see Christy sitting with Todd's folks. And when she sang a solo with the high school chorus and her name appeared with his last name, I felt like standing up and saying, "Hey, everybody, she's *my* daughter." It seems like I've given her up to another family.

But I am truly happy for her. I remember how lonely I was when I was a new bride. Tom was a college student, and I didn't know one other person in that strange college town a thousand miles away from home. It seemed as though I might drown in my tears.

How wonderful it is for them to be surrounded by two families and friends who love them. Surely such love must make their days richer and their nights more secure.

Lord, help me to be always thankful and never jealous. Keep me from trying to compete for their affection. Let me joyfully share Christy with her new family.

April 11

I do not want to be that awfulest of creatures, the "mother-in-law."

Today I interfered. It was impossible for me to keep quiet when I realized that the payments on the used car they were considering buying would surely outlast the car.

If only we could pass on to our children by osmosis the little bit of wisdom that we have gleaned from making mistakes. But I know that they are no different than we are—they need to learn so many things the hard way.

I must not try to rob them of life's greatest learning technique—experience. I remember our own early years of marriage. We didn't relish or appreciate sensible advice from our elders. Surprisingly, we lived through those years, and they should, too. I realize that to the young belongs the privilege of making mistakes.

Lord, keep me patient and quiet.

April 16

They've had to grow up so fast. In the coming months there will be more growth. There will be responsibilities, and challenges, and frustrations. They are engaged in the struggle of becoming.

But in becoming and growing there is change. Who will they be in five, ten, or twenty years? Will they grow together or apart? Will their interests serve to bind them or to separate?

> *Lord, for three years Christy and Todd have enjoyed doing many things together. Let them continue as each other's best friend with a shared zest for living. Let them have common interests. Especially unite them as they read Your Word and pray together. May Your presence in their lives be cement in their marriage.*
>
> *But, God, as they grow together give to each of them enough individuality to keep them interesting.*

April 17

This evening Todd was working, so Christy came to see us. She went with Tom and I and Phillip for a ride in the forest preserve.

We looked for deer and moose the way we used to. We pushed back the walls of time and reached for old memories. We watched the slanted rays of sunlight search the forest floor, saw a shrew scamper across the road, smelled the woods, and recalled other times.

We were glad to have her with us as if she were a little girl again. I felt blithely content as memories of the past mingled with the present.

I thank You, Lord, that we have good things to remember. Help us to do fun things with people we love. Give us tender moments. Fill our lives with gentleness and caring. Help us to cherish each day, because soon today will be tomorrow's yesterday.

Help us to live each day so we might gather in warm memories for our old age.

April 21

Today I watched Christy as she played on the grass with Phillip, and I became overwhelmed with old feelings.

She never had a chance to know anyone but Todd—to discover a world bigger than her own backyard. Since she was thirteen and he fifteen, he was always there caring for her and she loving him. It's like two flowers picked before they were barely budding. They never reached full bloom on the bush.

Why do I feel sad? They can bloom together. I can cast off my sadness because now they seem completely happy. I can tell she is content. She looks to her husband and waits for their child. They do things together. They swim, and play tennis, and celebrate life. I should be happy for them.

Again I ask You, Lord, help me not to resent Todd because he snatched Christy away from me before I was ready to give her up. Perhaps I would never be ready to let her go and there would be no man good enough.

He is a fine person with many noble qualities. Help me to love him as I love her. Help love to triumph over resentment.

April 28

I miss Christy. I see her often, but it's not the same. She stops in almost every day, but she comes as a woman, not as a girl demanding things. There are no demands left to be imposed on each other. It is so strange that we are free agents as we relate to each other. I am no longer the mother who asks her child to be obedient nor she the child who reminds me what a mother owes. Duty is gone and only love and friendship remain.

Is it the love of sixteen years that binds us now? We see each other because we care and are interested in what happens to each other.

Our relationship has a different quality. Quibbling and bickering have vanished. I don't know how it is with her, but I can't afford to be dominating or unpleasant. I might scare her away.

I do miss our old parent-child relationship because I was so sure of myself. But a new relationship is forming and I feel it is a better one, based on trust and caring rather than obligation. We are becoming more aware of each other's needs. I am getting to know the person behind her skin and she's beginning to see me as someone other than just "Mom."

Lord, continue with us now as we relate as equals.

May 7

Christy's wearing maternity clothes now. It seems so strange to see her this way. In my mind I still see her wearing her jeans and T-shirts. I still at times find myself wanting... wishing things to be the way they were. Why can't I completely accept her being married and pregnant?

She is happy. She's in love with married life and her husband. She likes being pregnant and wearing maternity clothes. She caresses her abdomen and longs for the life that grows inside of her.

Pregnancy seems to agree with her. She is vibrant and overflows with expectancy and contentment.

Her enthusiasm is contagious. I feel myself getting excited, too. I can't imagine what it will be like having a grandchild. I wonder who that little person will be? I can't wait to hold him or her.

Help me, Lord, to be happy for her and to share her anticipation and her joy.

May 22

I haven't lost Christy like I thought I would. She didn't depart from our lives and leave an aching void. Her first loyalty is to her husband, as it should be. But she still comes as a beloved daughter and walks in and out of our lives, scattering joy here and there. She comes and sprinkles laughter and spreads cheer, teases her little brother, and makes a father's heart glad. She caresses her abdomen because she plans to give us the joy of a grandchild.

We speak as one woman to another and have special things to talk about. She lets me help her. It used to be that she never needed help. Before I was considered hopelessly old-fashioned, but now I am worthy of the asking.

God, I am enjoying this new relationship. I thank You that my fears were for nothing. Let us continue enjoying each other. And, Lord, let me always know my boundaries.

May 24

Todd has decided to wait a year before he starts college. Christy told me that they both feel that a new baby, moving, his beginning college, and her transferring to a new high school would be too much for them to experience all at once. I think they have made a wise decision.

I am so happy I feel like laughing and singing because they will live here in town with us for yet another year. Christy will continue walking in and out of our lives. Her laughter will still vibrate throughout the town and in our living room. I can again hear her sing in the high school chorus, and she wants me to continue attending parent-teacher conferences. For another year she will be close by and we can enjoy her youth.

And that little baby will be here, too. We won't have to miss out on its growing. I wonder who it will be? When it smiles for the first time, we will come running. When it worries our daughter with a fever or a cough, we will be close by. What fun it will be to baby-sit, cuddle, and play with this baby who is coming into our lives. I'm so glad we won't miss out on its first year.

God, I thank You because life seems so good today.

May 26

Lord, Todd graduates tonight, and now living will be easier for him. I'm glad he is through with six hours of school followed by eight hours of work.

Be with him now as he graduates. He is standing at life's crossroads. Don't let him walk alone, but stay by his side and hold his hand when the going gets rough. And when life is good, let him remember Who it is that gives him life and breath, and health and wealth.

Todd doesn't seem to have any definite plans for what he will do or who he will become. But, nevertheless, help him to get on with the doing of becoming. Be with him as he explores his future. Help him to consider the alternatives and give him wisdom as he sorts out priorities. Give him insight as to who he is and who he wants to become. Make him aware of what he needs in life to feel fulfilled. Pave his pathway with right decisions.

Now as he graduates let him see himself as Your child and help him to seek out Your purpose in his life.

Lord, go with him and bless him so that he might become a blessing.

June 6

Christy has started working at a motel coffee shop for the summer. It is important to her that she helps with the family finances.

I am happy that they are diligent about making it on their own. I am glad they have an independent spirit and that they have assumed responsibility for themselves.

There will be many expenses when the baby is born and when winter comes. I hope they won't be too depressed when the bills are larger than their income.

God, give them wisdom in money matters, but don't let their striving to get ahead rob them of life's joy.

And, Lord, as she starts work, keep her from being tired and let her quick smile brighten a weary traveler's day.

June 11

I feel thankful today because Todd has a new job. He won't have to pump gas at night and on weekends anymore. I guess I won't be seeing so much of Christy now that he'll be home when she is. But I am happy for her. They need to spend their leisure hours with each other.

I'm glad about his new job. He'll be setting ads for his father's newspaper. I hope he will have a happy working relationship with his father.

Lord, bless their leisure hours. Enrich their evening hours and weekends. Let them examine the lingering sunset. As they ride their bikes on a country lane, give to them the trill of the meadowlark and the fragrance of wild lilies and clover.

Bless them as they worship together on Sunday morning and visit his grandmother on Sunday afternoon. As they share their leisure, let them experience joy in living.

June 14

Christy and Todd moved out of that house that shakes in the wind, and into a cozy little trailer.

I am happy today because they are excited about their new home. It fits them. I can tell they feel comfortable and secure now, because they spend more time in their own home.

They are becoming a family. They seem to be feeling and thinking together. They don't spend so much time at their parental homes now. Instead, they sit inside of their own four walls and look to each other for companionship and security. I miss Christy not coming around so much, but isn't this the way it's supposed to be?

I thank You, Lord, that their home is becoming the most comfortable place in the world for them to be. It is wonderful the way You provide.

June 23

What a beautiful thing young love is. It is vivacious, yet tender. They are each other's best friend, sharing their lives at church and on the tennis court. They picnic, and swim, and tease each other.

What a powerful thing youth is. It is optimistic and enthusiastic. It holds the future in its hands and soars above the world. We see stumbling blocks that threaten harmony, prosperity, and progress. But youth sees only visions of well-carried-out plans and goals already reached.

Their hopes and dreams belong to each other. Especially the hope she carries within her body. Is it the excitement and anticipation of their baby that draws them so close?

How can I regret Christy's childhood gone when I see such happiness?

Keep them, Lord, ever in Your presence and chasing dreams. Let neither providing for bread nor making their own kingdom keep them from Your kingdom.

June 29

I haven't seen Christy for days—just a beep of the horn as she drives by, and a quick "hello" in the store. She used to come by almost twice a day.

Can it be that she doesn't need us anymore? Do her husband, and home and friends satisfy her so much? Does she no longer need to come and feel familiar things? Does she have enough strength in her own home so that she needn't come to borrow any?

Is her husband her sufficiency? Does he fill her vacant moments and keep her glad?

Isn't this the way it's supposed to be? Isn't this what I asked for?

Help me, Lord, to accept the rhythm of life. A child grows, and leaves, and becomes.
Let me rejoice.

Anticipation

July 18

Christy grows larger now and I am so afraid for her. She's too young to go through childbirth.

The doctor said because of her small size he may have to take the baby by Caesarean section. But because she has been so active and limber, he would like her to go into labor and see what happens. Then if the delivery doesn't proceed normally, they will do a section.

I wish she didn't have to go through this. I wish the baby were already born. I am afraid she will be in labor for many hours, and then the doctors will do a Caesarean section.

Lord, keep her safe. Don't let her suffer too much. Protect her from danger and grant to them a healthy child.

August 7

It looks as if I am going to eat my words. How many times have I told my children I will never baby-sit my grandchildren. But this is different. Christy could never finish high school if I didn't.

I don't know if I am ready for a baby to interrupt my freedom, or my carefree schedule, or my quiet hours. But I want to do this joyfully.

My friends seem to delight in their grandchildren. They are completely overwhelmed by an infant's smile and a small head pressed against their breast.

What will this child bring into my life? Will it make my sluggish heart beat faster? Will it soothe the pain of growing older? Will it color my world with pastels and bright colors? Will it add wonder to Christmas? Will it make this house vibrate with new laughter?

Yes, I am ready for this kind of joy. The bassinet awaits a grandchild, and so does my heart.

August 30

Summer is over. The baby is due any day and Christy is back in school. When she talked to the principal about starting now and taking off a few weeks when the baby comes, he said, "Why not? The teachers do." I am glad we are living in an age when child-bearing is considered a normal and natural part of life.

I am happy that she's getting started with her studies before the baby arrives. But she must be sticky hot and aching heavy while she tries to sit in those desks. And I can imagine her trying to rush through those overcrowded hallways to get from class to class.

God, I thank You for her spirit. Help her to keep trying even when she feels like quitting. It would be natural for her interest in school to wane when she's so excited about becoming a mother. I pray that You will give her enough energy to be a loving wife, a mother, and an excellent student.

Let her continue to achieve academically. I know it won't be easy for her, God, but I pray that You will help her to make it through these last two years of high school.

Equip her, Lord, so that she might serve her family well, and then the world.

September 3

I don't understand myself. I'm becoming a compulsive spender, buying things for that baby. I don't know why I am finding such joy in buying and touching little things. When I hold a little shirt, I wonder who will be in it.

Am I enjoying this so much because money was so scarce when our first baby was born? Or has excitement overtaken me because once again a baby is coming into our lives? Perhaps I have caught a disease called "grandmother fever." I have been acting very strangely lately. I even sewed a baby quilt. Everyone knows sewing by choice and not duty is strange behavior for me.

I am glad Christy and Todd allow me to participate in this great event in their lives. They seem happy when I come with something for the baby.

When the baby arrives, Lord, help me to remember that I am only the grandmother and my daughter is the mother.

September 5

Today is Christy's due date. All is ready.

A nursery awaits a baby. The crib is made, diapers are stacked, and a teddy bear watches with wide eyes from a corner on a shelf. Tiny, sweet-smelling shirts and sleepers and sweaters are folded in place, and a music box waits to unwind its lullabye.

Christy and Todd are ready. They wonder at the miracle of life and have hope in the future. Their longing arms wait to cradle their own firstborn. They say they can't imagine having a baby that belongs to them.

Todd's folks and we... are ready. They already know the joy of grandchildren, and we wait for this new kind of happiness. We are two families eager to greet a new member. That child can't know that so many of us are waiting to love it.

Lord, that baby has to be born soon. So now I ask You to be with Christy and Todd. Keep her safe and him calm and bless them with a healthy child.

September 7

Lately I feel like a busybody, always checking on Christy. It's amazing how many excuses I've been coming up with to stop by their trailer. And in the middle of the night, I walk out in the yard to look down the street at the hospital to see if their car is parked in front.

Last night I just "happened" to go bike-riding at eleven o'clock. They came home from a movie just as I was pedaling by their place and I felt silly. I asked her how she was and she said she was feeling fine. They have to know what I'm up to and are probably laughing at me.

I wish that baby would be born. I constantly feel excited, exhilarated, and so concerned. My hours and minutes are filled with thinking about her and the baby. Those two even interrupt my sleep.

I am happy that Christy and Todd share with me these exciting and intimate days. They say they don't mind our coming around. However, I hope I have sense enough to know if I am becoming a pest. And I don't want to barge in on any sacred, personal moments of their lives.

September 12

I find myself walking around nervous these days. A whole week has gone by since her due date, and she grows so large.

I will be glad when this is over. Her husband is anxious, too. Why am I acting this way? Young women give birth to babies every day. She abounds with energy and is in excellent health. It is silly for me to be afraid for her.

Why am I acting this way? Why am I nervous and anxious when I know God is here? How can I fret when I have called on His name?

Lord, I leave my fears and cares with You. I trust You to take care of her and to keep her safe.

September 13

Today all I can think about is the baby. It is strange how much I've noticed babies lately. I've been looking at them with new eyes. They are so innocent. I'd forgotten how an infant's smile can melt hearts of stone; how a giggle can penetrate the deep recesses of gloom.

How can a being so small beckon people to abandon dreariness and embrace life with laughter?

I wonder who he or she will be? How excited we will be when it smiles for the first time, when it discovers its hands, gets a tooth, and learns to walk!

It seems like a hundred years since a wee one has brightened our lives. Right now all of the people in our house are eager to love an infant. We wait for joy.

In the middle of the afternoon Christy went to the hospital, but it wasn't like we all planned. Nobody sat with her and helped her time her contractions. She had no labor or pain—just a gush of blood and a quick trip to the hospital.

The doctor told us that the baby was in distress and its heartbeat was disappearing fast. An anesthesiologist hurried to the hospital and they said they would do a Caesarean section as soon as surgery could be set up.

The doctor didn't say it, but I knew Christy was in danger, too. At first all I could think about was how dear she is to us, and to her husband, and to his family. Then I desperately hoped and longed and prayed that that little baby would live, too. How we all had been longing to hold it and love it. I tried to tell God that I knew the kids would be good parents; that they seemed ready for parenthood.

When they wheeled her into surgery, the doctor said he couldn't hear the baby's heartbeat anymore. I knew that meant that the baby's oxygen supply was cut off, and if it lived there would be a possibility of brain damage. I felt their marriage couldn't endure that, so I began asking God to let the baby live only if it could be healthy.

It all seemed so strange. How could anything go so wrong that had seemed so right just an hour before?

Todd's folks and members of our families sat with us in the little hospital room. We didn't talk to each other—just sat there silently pleading with God.

The Baby

The doctor came in and told us that Christy came through the surgery in good shape, but the baby was dead.

The baby is dead. I have hard feelings. If only the doctor would have done the Caesarean earlier, like he had talked about doing. Then the baby would be alive and healthy. But I can't blame him when I know how serious major surgery is compared to normal delivery. No one could predict that the placenta would separate before the baby was born.

Then I think if only she could have miscarried. Then we could have kept them from marrying and she'd still be living in our home. Is that the reason she didn't miscarry at three months? Because I am so unyielding? If we had kept them from marrying, perhaps I would be spending my hours trying to keep them apart. Perhaps my daughter and I would be hating each other instead of loving.

Lord, I feel confused at the pattern of our lives. But let me accept the fact that Your ways are not our ways. Let me realize that Your wisdom is greater than our passion.

There is so much pain. I feel flat, empty, void. I saw the baby. She was perfectly formed, beautiful, and dead. I ache. Life has so many cruel turns. We expected joy.

During those nine long months, Christy radiated with good health. Her cheeks had a flush of pink and she was lithe of limb. She was careful about her diet and got plenty of exercise. She was exuberant and so expectant. How could anything go so wrong?

I had prayed. So did the others. Didn't God hear us? We all sat there praying so hard. Was He even aware of us?

I know He was there keeping Christy safe. The doctor said she might have bled to death in an hour or the amniotic fluid might have mixed with her blood and poisoned her.

I know that God was in control. It is no coincidence that the doctor was in the hospital on a bright Saturday afternoon in September; or that the surgical nurse happened to be on duty; or that the anesthesiologist from the neighboring town was at home; he might have been fishing—or that the other doctor who was not even on call was at home; he might have gone somewhere with his children. And it wasn't a coincidence that just yesterday afternoon I thought to say to Christy, "If you have any red discharge, that means trouble and you should get to the hospital fast."

I know that it didn't just happen that Christy was in surgery just thirty-five minutes after the hemorrhaging started. God was close by guarding and protecting.

But why did He let the baby slip away?

September 15

Why does a rosebud fall from a bush, never to bloom? Why does a young bird fall from its nest, never to fly? Why does a young tree blow over in the forest while others remain strong?

Did God will for this little one to die? Did He want that death should deny it breath? Does He delight in our grief?

No. I know that death and suffering are intruders in His creation. I know that it is His desire that we experience life and happiness.

Is it because evil is yet a reality, stalking the earth until Jesus comes and takes us home to eternal joy.

Lord, we suffer now with heavy hearts. I ask You to take this pain and use it.

September 16

Today a tear rolled down Christy's cheek and she whispered, "Maybe God wants us to be more mature before we're parents."

I ached so much for her that I could hardly hold my tears inside of me. She can't even cry because her abdomen is sore and she is so weak.

I spoke to the doctor today, and he reassured us that it is highly unlikely this could happen again in another pregnancy. But he said she will have to have any future children by Caesarean section.

They are already thinking about next time. I feel bad for her that she has to go through surgery to have a baby. But I am thankful that she is alive and there can be a next time.

God, comfort her now and give her a happy tomorrow.

September 17

Christy's arms are empty, her abdomen sore, and her heart is aching.

From the corridors comes a cry of someone else's newborn infant and a lone tear rolls down her pale cheek. There is milk in her breast, too, but no baby to suck.

Does she wonder if she can face another day? Or does she challenge the hours because she knows today will pass and a happier tomorrow comes from the eastern horizon.

Does she feel she has disappointed her husband and the rest of us? She had hoped to delight us and make our hearts happy.

God, I ask You to heal her pain, soothe her aching heart, and give her courage.
Use our love to cushion her hurt.

September 18

Todd. He aches so. The pain oozes from him. His baby is gone and his wife lies wan and weak.

He stands by her side and caresses her hand. They are bound by love and pain.

He expected joy but is laid low with grief. But he praises God because he still has his wife.

Comfort him, Lord. Surround him with Your love and give him strength.
Be with them, God, as they work through their loss.

September 19

Why them? Why has God allowed this to happen? They seemed to be so ready to be parents. And we were two families ready to love that little baby.

Why? Is it because their relationship needs strengthening? I already see them drawing closer. Together they share their grief and are tender with each other.

Does God want to draw them nigh unto himself? Is He saying to them, "Give Me your sorrows and your cares, and I will comfort you and strengthen you and supply all your needs"?

Did God let the baby die because He wanted to salvage the raw material of their young lives? Would a baby keep them from realizing their talents and potential?

Because of their pain and sorrow, will they be more sensitive to others who suffer?

Because of their grief, will their joy be greater?

Lord, I know that pain and death are never Your will, but use their suffering to make them better people.

September 20

Christy went home to their trailer today. I had asked her if she wanted Todd's mother and me to take the nursery down and pack away all of the baby's things. She said, "No, we will do it together."

So together they work through their pain. The teddy bear's wide eyes now stare at the bottom of a box. Next to it is the music box whose lullabye never delighted an infant. Its strains only fell on our hopeful ears.

They packed away the tiny shirts, and socks and sweaters and diapers along with pieces of hope for the future and regrets for the little person who never got to be.

Did tears help them with their work or did anguish stay inside their hearts and threaten to crush their soul?

God, be with these two young people whom I love. Bless them as they struggle with hurt. Help them to walk this path of pain. Show Christy and Todd how much You love them.

September 22

I finally feel like I'm beginning to really love the boy who married my daughter—even as I love her. That resentment I've felt is gone.

> *God, I thank You for Christy and Todd and the lessons they have taught me. They've made me put my pride in my pocket, and together we've drunk the sweet wine of forgiveness.*
>
> *I thank You for them and their lesson of love. They hold each other in highest regard and care about the rest of us. I thank You for staying with them as they work out this first experience with pain. I thank You that they are working out their grief together and have learned to call Your name. And they discovered Your name is Love.*
>
> *I thank You because they have found You in the midst of misery. They have found out how merciful You are and they praise You.*
>
> *I praise You for working in all of our lives. It is so strange how You can take the events we would choose to erase from our lives and use them for good. So I praise You when I hurt, when I am disappointed, and when things seem rotten, because You are here. You take the bane of our existence and use it to Your glory.*

September 24

Lord, I feel like celebrating again. I cannot celebrate pain or loss but I celebrate Your faithfulness.

In the midst of our misery and tears You come to comfort. You send people into our lives to bring us Your love.

You are too wonderful, Lord. You rejoice when we are happy and show pity when we hurt. You do not leave us to languish but interrupt our pain. You take the awful things in our lives and put them to good use.

Is there anyone like You, O Lord? Who are we that You should even be aware of us? You do not live in the lofty heavens, but You walk our streets and enter into our lives. You are aware of our sighings and our bliss.

I celebrate today because You know us and have called us by name.

Epilogue

As this little book goes to press, Christy and Todd are celebrating their sixth anniversary. In many ways it has been a long six years. They have known times of great joy and other times of almost unbearable pain. Yes, they have known even separation and reconciliation.

I am not trying to excuse them or defend them. I suppose, naturally speaking, that grave problems were almost inevitable. But "naturally speaking" does not include God. And He was there with unimaginable resources to help them through the difficult times in their marriage if only they had known then how to let Him. In spite of those dark days when it looked as if the marriage was not going to last, they did experience growth and they are learning how to trust God for each other and their marriage.

Sixteen months after they lost their baby, Todd and Christy had another baby girl when Christy was a senior in high school. Christy went on to nurses' training and now works as a registered nurse. The three of them live two blocks from us and continue to walk in and out of our lives and give us joy.

As we look back, we can't help but wonder about our decisions. Would they have been the same if we could make them over again? I suppose it depends on how far back one looks. As a mother with a good, open relationship with my daughter, I wish now that I had taken some risks with that relationship and given more firm direction in her life.

But considering the circumstances six years ago,

I think we made the right choice. Christy and Todd think so too.

They would be the first to admit that their marriage has looked pretty hopeless at times. Those periods were hard on Todd's parents and on us, too. But once again we learned to leave these matters in God's hands. The sense of responsibility for them changed from decision-making to quiet concern, little bits of advice sparingly given, and lots of prayer. Together they have sought counseling and have learned that a good marriage takes a great deal of work.

Since this is as much my story as Christy's and Todd's, I want to thank God for His care and concern for me, too, over these years. Tom and I continue our celebration because God walks with us and shows us in many ways His love to us and to our family.

Other Helpful Reading for Families, from Bethany House Publishers:

THE CHRISTIAN FAMILY, Larry Christenson—A million and a quarter copies sold! A basic guidebook for families.

BUILDING RESPECT, RESPONSIBILITY, AND SPIRITUAL VALUES IN YOUR CHILD, Mike Phillips—How to develop a plan for raising your children into godly adults.

DEVELOPING SPIRITUALLY SENSITIVE CHILDREN, Olive Alexander—The Golden Rule for parents: do unto your children as you would have done to you if you were their size and age.

HOW TO RAISE GOOD KIDS, Barbara Cook—An optimistic, enthusiastic mother shares some refreshingly simple principles from the Bible.

HOW TO RAISE YOUR CHILDREN FOR CHRIST, Andrew Murray—A classic which develops principles from all the families in the Bible from Genesis to Hebrews.

SPANKING—WHY? WHEN? HOW?, Roy Lessin—Important truths for every parent confused about today's permissiveness and unsure about the Bible's teaching on discipline.

WHICH WAY THE FAMILY?, Larry Christenson—A booklet containing practical, down-to-earth help for the family from one of America's leading authorities on family life.

THE GREAT DATE WAIT...AND OTHER HAZARDS, William L. Coleman—A devotional book for teens, preteens, and their parents, covering all the relationships which face young people—from "little brothers" to "the big date."